A BUFF

Gimme jimmy.

Mayor James D. Griffin
In His Own Words and Pictures

By Steve Cichon
With a Forward by The Griffin Children

ISBN 978-0-982739-1-5

Published by Buffalo Stories LLC and staffannouncer.com

Table of Contents

i. Forward

"Always leave a place better than you found it."

-advice often offered by James D. Griffin

If you're reading this and only knew our father from what you read in the news, you're probably going to be surprised.

As we were growing up, he was the mayor, sure. He'd even remind us with an occasional, "Because I'm the Mayor, that's why." (To which we'd joke back that he wasn't the mayor at home.)

But mostly, he was our dad.

He hated when we didn't have money. He always gave us a couple of bucks for our pockets when we went out. "Have fun and watch yourself. Just remember whatever you do reflects on this family."

Sometimes we'd be watching TV and he'd turn it off, put on a record, and call our mom into dance with him. She'd laugh, and he'd tell us to watch "what a graceful dancer your mother is."

He'd tell us that we just have to give people a break; that you never know what's going on in someone's life. That you can never go wrong with being nice to someone. It doesn't cost you anything, and you might make someone's day better. That's the same advice his dad gave him.

With a smile, he'd ask, "Margie what the hell is wrong with these kids? Who'd want any of you three?"

Around report card time, he'd say, "There's going to be an ass-kicking contest, and you three are the only contestants."

We knew there wasn't much we could get away with. "Don't bullshit a bullshitter," he'd say.

But he was our dad, and he was the Mayor.

4

What was normal for us might not have been for any other kid.

Our phone number was always in the phone book. At very young ages, we learned to take proper phone messages, even if they were sometimes written in crayon. We always gave Dad his messages first thing through the door.

During a snow storm our phone would ring almost non-stop with people telling us their street needed plowing.

We got pretty good at fielding these calls. Where exactly is this street? Are there cars parked on the street? One side or both sides? Can you tell your neighbors to move their cars so the plows can get through?

Armed with all the right information, we'd call the streets department and let them know.

Other than citizens with quality of life issues, the other group that called most often were reporters.

Some we knew we could hang up on, but some would be welcomed into our home for interviews over and over again.

Our mother was always a gracious hostess for reporters like Nona Barbie, Marie Rice, Carol Crissey, Don Postles, Jacquie Walker, Rich Kellman, Rich Newberg, and so many others.

When we were little, we'd bring out cups of coffee for the reporters and cameramen, and we were allowed to sit in our footie pajamas and listen, so long as we stayed quiet.

Fielding Questions from Channel 4 chief photographer Don Yearke

The phone wasn't the only means of communication we were familiar with… Our dad always had a two-way radio in the car, and just about anywhere we drove, there was something to be called in. A car needed to be towed off the street. There was garbage dumped somewhere. A light or sign was broken. The city radio code was "M-100."

He'd call it in, asking the name of the employee taking the call. We'd take the same route home, to make sure that M-100 was corrected. We usually left early for events and took city streets most places, driving through the neighborhoods-- sometimes to look at an address or intersection or street there'd been a complaint about. Dad liked to see for himself, and better be able to handle the situation.

Occasionally, the complaints were about us. We behaved as we normally did—badly-- and City Hall was really like a second home.

Once we got kicked out of Common Council chambers when we were messing around. But mostly, we'd go visit Uncle Tom's office, where he had whistle pops. We'd stop to see Aunt Donna, who worked in Parks, too. Or we'd pretend we could type really fast, and only occasionally jam up a typewriter. Or we'd copy our hands and faces (or other body parts, Tommy) on the Xerox machine.

We'd also make dad a cup of tea in the kitchen that connected to his office. Or we'd go into the file drawer and pull out an envelope of Cup-O-Soup to make for ourselves.

While our animal-like behavior didn't bother Dad, our mom far more aware. Like the time Governor Hugh Carey invited our family to the Governor's Mansion soon after Dad was elected.

We were there with the Governor's grandkids, and to hear mom tell it, if she could have reached us, she would have torn us limb from limb.

We were hammering the keys on a piano, sliding down a long, elegant flight of stairs on our stomachs, and generally just running around this grand house and loving every minute of it.

No matter whether Dad was meeting the Governor or the President or whomever, most nights, we had dinner as a family. He'd tell us to help mom clean up, and always thank her for a wonderful meal.

"Thanks Margie, that really hit the spot," he'd say, always sitting down to a family dinner.

And although the phone rang a lot, he rarely took a call during dinner. He sat next to the phone, and would usually answer himself, saying that he was sitting down to dinner with Margie and the kids, and to please call back in twenty minutes.

If the fact that our dad was a kind, gracious, enthusiastic man comes as a bit of a surprise to you, we're happy to share not only our stories, but a few that we've learned along the way as well.

We've always known about his warm and giving heart, but in the time since our Dad died, we've heard dozens of stories and learned so much more about him through people he quietly helped through the years.

At Dad's wake, there was a Buffalo Police Officer who told us about how her father died on her 12th birthday, and our dad organized a fundraiser to help keep her and her family in school.

Sometimes he'd disappear from his grandkids' baseball games. We'd get ticked and wonder where he had to go that was so important. Well, we found out that long after he retired from City Hall, he was sponsoring baseball teams around the city for kids who wouldn't otherwise have the chance to play.

He bought the equipment, got to know the kids, helped coach. At that point, he knew those other kids needed him more than his grandkids, who had great support and love.

As you can see, our dad was more than the caricature he was made out to be sometimes in the press. We hope that as you flip through the following pages, you get to know our dad like we knew him.

Make sure you look at the smile in almost every photo. That's the guy we know and love.

All of the photos in this book were ones that he and our mom collected through the years, from both the mayor's office and our family albums.

The words are almost all his too, recorded during his over 50 years of public service for the city and people he loved.

As Dad would always say: Good luck, good health, and God bless,

Maureen, Megan, and Tom Griffin
August, 2013

Holding newborn grandchild, 1996.

ii. Grab a Six Pack

In his time, Jim Griffin was either loved or hated. It was hard to be ambivalent about such a larger-than-life, over-the-top figure who invariably told you exactly what was on his mind.

But as we now count the time since he was mayor in decades, as a city, our thoughts about Mayor Griffin have softened around the edges a bit and become a little foggy. That's for those of us who have first hand memories. A 30 year old might not have any personal memories of the mayor at all.

There is, however, one specific memory that's gotten stronger and clearer through the years as it's taken on a life of its own. It's a phrase, a quote, a moment in time memory that has become *who Jimmy Griffin is* for many people. He often said it would be on his tombstone.

"Stay inside and grab a six pack."

It's the perfect Buffalo phrase. It involves snow, *our ability to handle snow*, beer, *our ability to handle beer*, and it was delivered by our favorite grain-scoopin'-gin-mill-owner-turned mayor from down-in-the-Ward.

It is all those things, but to take a look back at the quote, and how and why it was born, gives an insight into the Jim Griffin's time as mayor and life in Buffalo in the 1980s.

It was the Blizzard of 1985. Three feet of snow in three days. A driving ban in Buffalo. Governor Cuomo declared a state of emergency. Mayor Griffin was not only mayor, but acting Streets Commissioner as well. He was at the Broadway barns coordinating snow removal efforts. He was riding plows.

He was driving the streets, a two-way radio in hand, to make sure the storm of the decade was being handled better than the most recent big storm in January, 1977, which left 11 dead in the city of Buffalo.

To be certain, being in the middle of whatever needed to be done was the way he operated. He was always clearly in charge and always wanted to have a good handle on what was going on in his city; especially as the city was in the grips of a potential disaster. Taking the story this far, the phrase means what it has come to mean.

"Stay inside and grab a six pack."

It goes beyond that though.

In a storyline that was very familiar in Buffalo during the 80s, Mayor Griffin was running the Streets Department because there was no Streets Commissioner. There was no Streets Commissioner because of a stalemate between the mayor and the Common Council.

Over the course of a year, the Mayor nominated Joseph Scinta as the Commissioner of Street Sanitation over a dozen times. Over a dozen times, Scinta was rejected by the common council.

After 5 rejections, in November, 1984, Griffin was almost prophetic in telling people that they need to "blame their councilmen when the snow was piling up."

Frustrated and mystified, the Mayor told residents to call their councilmen, and tell them to "start acting like men instead of acting like boys."

As the elected Chief Executive of the city, Griffin's philosophy was that the people elected him to do what he thought was best for Buffalo. In doing what he thought was for the betterment of the city, he didn't like obstruction. Especially when it came with what he saw as ulterior motives beyond having the city's best at heart.

Perhaps the best proof of Jim Griffin's love for his city and holding close its best interests came with that late January, 1985 blast of snow.

A political operative might have thought with three feet of snow immobilizing the city that the feared and predicted emergency was cause for an "I told you so" news conference. Not Griffin.

As the snow fell, and he personally coordinated the snow fighting efforts, Griffin demurred on questions about the Common Council and their rejection of his Streets Commissioner choice.

In fact, with joy, he strapped on his boots and his two-way radio to show the country—and Buffalo itself—how we handle the sort of adversity and snow that would leave many others crippled.

With WGR's Stan Roberts

This wasn't going to be the Blizzard of '77. He was going to get things cleaned up his way, with a can-do Buffalo spirit.

And it was with a smile that several times over the days of the storm and the clean-up, Griffin told reporters his advice for the homebound people of Western New York:

Stay home and grab a six-pack.

He also added that if you can't clear your walk or driveway, that you should give a kid a few bucks to do it for you. More perfect advice, meant to keep the whole city moving. Keep kids busy, get the place cleaned up.

The mayor received high marks across the board for the way the city handled the Blizzard of '85, especially the clearing of roads and the relatively quick lifting of the city's driving ban.

Initially. But it was, after all, an election year.

By summer, during a debate with opponent (and Common Council President) George Arthur, the mayor was put on defensive about the overall snow removal plan.

"When you get 45 inches of snow," explained the mayor, "I challenge anyone to come up with a plan that works."

Opponents also tried to gain traction revisiting that advice Griffin gave which seemed to many, "unbecoming a mayor."

Yes, in 1985, the "six pack" quote was campaign fodder meant to prove Hizzoner's lack of decorum and behavior unbecoming the Chief Executive of the second largest city in the State of New York.

As you might expect, he stood tall.

"I'm proud of the statement. You get a blizzard here in Buffalo, you have to get off the street. I'll probably give the advice again. I don't see anything wrong with it. It was a humorous statement."

So the next time those big wet snowflakes are unloading outside your window…or you're not sure heading into work is the best idea as you strain to push 15 inches of snow off your windshield… Joyfully think of ol'Jimmy Griffin when you decide to stay home and enjoy some beverages.

But remember that even in giving the most resounding widely accepted advice in Buffalo's history, our most loved—and most hated—mayor had to take it on the chin to give it.

It's with that in mind that this book took the shape that it did.

The Griffin family has hundreds and hundreds of photos of the mayor in action.

From 1978 to 1993, just about every one of those actions was questioned. Most of the questions were answered by Jim Griffin himself.

It's quite clear that James D. Griffin knew exactly what he was doing and did it without apology or compromise.

Instead of allowing history and the passage of time to rewrite his motivations or to explain what he was doing in a more modern context, with this book, we present Jimmy Griffin in two unapologizing ways.

One, in his own photos—the ones he and his family saved for posterity.

Two, in his own words—Mostly the ones he spoke to reporters that were saved for posterity in print and on audio and video tape, including many he spoke to me directly when I was a reporter for WBEN Radio.

This is Jimmy Griffin the way he would have wanted to be seen. Just him. No varnish or primping. Take it or leave it.

-Steve Cichon
August, 2013

With Carl Paladino and family

The Mayor and his dad

1. From "The Ward"

Brother Tom & Jim Griffin. 1940s

"I hauled potatoes during the Depression. I worked summers at the Elk Street Market unloading Budweiser kegs, I worked at McMahon's store on South Park and Hamburg for 25 cents an hour when I was in seventh grade at St. Brigid's. I never worried about what job I had, so long as I made a buck."

It was a place where most people were on the edge of welfare. Many of the people worked as scoopers trying to get enough money to last through the winter. That was before unemployment insurance, and welfare was something you looked down on, something you took right before going to the poor house.

–Mayor Griffin on growing up in the old First Ward

St. Brigid's Class of 1943. Jim Griffin is second row from the top, second from the right.

Jim Griffin, middle row, second from right. 1940s

Mayor Griffin on "The Ward" —

"This is not a geographical area, it's a state of mind. We learned something in the neighborhood. We learned that loyalty is number one, and that standing up for your rights is number two."

"I don't think there's anybody who loves Buffalo more than I do. I'm honest with people. If I don't like somebody, they know it. I'm not phony. I'd rather punch somebody. I'm not going to be nice to a person who I don't think is a nice person. I've always done that. I made decisions. Some were good, some weren't too good, but at least I made a decision."

Jim Griffin, middle 1940s

"If you've been working hard in the feed mill all day, throwin' hundred pound bags around, and afterward you're drinkin' in some gin mill, and you run into some characters, the only way out is to fight. If you don't, you're yellow. It's the same thing in politics. Sometimes you have to assert yourself or people'll think you're indecisive."

-Mayor Griffin on First Ward justice

"I'm honest and down-to-earth. I like to think I have a sense of humor-- and common sense."

21

"I worked in a store after school when I was 12. I always played a lot of sports. I quit South Park High School as a sophomore. I went to work in the grain elevators. I was 16 at the time, but that was during the war. They didn't question your age too much.

Pretty rough work. The first couple weeks your arms and back would be sore, throwing the shovel.

You'd wear a mask on your mouth because of the grain dust. Sometimes you didn't wear it because it was uncomfortable. You'd wash the dust down with a couple of beers at noontime.

I was laid off from the scooping job, so finished High School at Our Lady of Victory High School in Lackawanna. Sister DeLaSalle let me take senior subjects so I could graduate in a year; graduated 1948.

Anything I've accomplished in life I owe to the great nuns at St. Brigid's and Our lady of Victory."

Jim Griffin, center, top row. 1940s

"My dad never made much money, but he'd take us down to Sullivan playground at South Park and Mackinaw every day to hit flies. He was a good athlete. His nickname was "Rocko." Years later, when I was running for State Senate, people would tell me, 'I'm voting for you because you're Rocko's kid.' I used to shoot craps in that playground, too."

"Some guys let power go to their heads. I hope it hasn't changed me. I've tried to keep my old friends, in and out of politics. Power is something God gives you, and you have a responsibility to use it in a certain way."

"I joined the army back in 1951, in February, in the Korean War. It probably wasn't a war like the Second World War, but I was glad I defended my country. I really enjoyed it, too. You'd be amazed how many people you meet and places you go. "

Mayor James D. Griffin in His Own Words and Pictures

After enlisting in the US Army in 1951, Griffin became a paratrooper and an officer. He saw combat in Korea with the Fifth Regimental Combat Team.

Griffin was a proud son of "The Ward," and proud of his Irish heritage. But not too proud.

"I'm not a professional Irishman. I love Ireland, been there three times. But if it was that great, my grandfather would still be over there. There's no other country in the world like the United States."

Jim Griffin was a railroad engineer and a tavern owner as he began a life in public service. Some advice learned around the gin mill is universally true...

"You don't get up and go to the bathroom when it's your turn to buy the round. You can't have short arms and long pockets."

2. The Family Man

Jim & Margie Griffin, married 40 years.

Rocko Griffin's Kids: Jim, Tom Jr, Tom "Rocko" Griffin Sr, Joe, Donna Griffin-Gasuik

The Mayor, his siblings, and their father.

Jim Griffin on his parents.

"My mom was great. She was a great cook. She was more outgoing than my father. "

"My dad was probably the best father a kid could have. He coached my brother Tommy, my brother Joe, and me in sports. He was a real good athlete, a heck of a lot better that I ever thought of being. And he never made much money. He worked for 50 years for Beals, McCarthy, and Rogers hardware store. I think he missed three days work in 50 years. If there was an idol in my life, it was my father."

Two Tom Griffins. Above: The Mayor's father sits in the Mayor's City Hall office chair. Tom Griffin proudly referred to his son as "my son the mayor." The Mayor referred to his dad as "my buddy." The senior Mr. Griffin died in 1991 at the age of 86. Below: Oldest Griffin brother Tom, Jr, was a role model, confidant, and Parks Commissioner for Mayor Griffin.

The Griffin Family relaxes, 1970

Hizzoner the Master of Ceremonies, with brother Tom

Grant Street Christmas Parade, 1980

Mr. & Mrs. James D. Griffin on their wedding day at Our Lady of Perpetual Help, 1968.

"We always knew each other. She lived on Tennessee Street all her life and we both went to OLV. I used to see her going to work every day at National Gypsum. I'd be watching through the window of a neighborhood tavern." - on knowing Mrs. Griffin

"Sixteen years is a long time to be in a fishbowl."

-Marge Griffin, on her time as Buffalo's First Lady, moments after Mayor Griffin announced he wouldn't be seeking a 5th term. 1993.

"I just remember Dad turning off the television and putting on a record when we were little. He'd call my mom into the family room and ask her to dance. She would laugh and always say okay. He would tell us to watch "what a graceful dancer your mother is." He'd say he could not dance before he met our mom. They would dance one or two songs, and we all used to laugh...."

-Maureen Griffin Tomczak

The Griffins dance in their Dorrance Avenue living room

"She was always very private, but also recognized the many people who supported her and our father for so many years. While she was private, most people recognized the strong influence that she had on our father throughout his career. They loved each other and they had great fun together. They loved to laugh and tell stories with the many friends they gathered throughout their busy life. "

-The Griffin Children on their mother

"The entire job is tough on my family. Tough on my wife Margie, she's my advisor and my friend. If there was ever going to be a priest who was going to be female, she'd hear my confession, for cryin' out loud."

"That's the tough part, being away from the family. Almost every Saturday, as part of the Mayor's job, I'm out talking some place, doing something that involves the city. My family makes an awful lot of sacrifices because I'm mayor, but the kids don't know any better. They've all been born since I was a State Senator."

Well, that I was a good father, a good husband, and a good son. And that I did the best I could.

-Mayor Griffin, on what he'd like to accomplish in life

"They're my legacy to the city. That and being a good mayor."

-Mayor Griffin on his kids, Maureen, Megan, and Tom.

Mayor Griffin's three oldest grandchildren, John, Joe, and Grace, pose with the city's official portrait of their grandfather at City Hall.

41

"They're good kids, they work hard. They make their mother and father very proud of them."
-Mayor Griffin talking about his children.

Celebrating victory with Megan, 1977

Megan and Tommy Griffin raiding the fridge outside their father's office. City Hall was like a second home to the Griffin kids growing up.

Proud father takes daughter Maureen down the aisle, 1995.

Proud Grandpa, 1996.

Holding grandson Joe

"I always have time for the kids"
- Mayor Griffin

Said of his kids, but true of his grandkids as well....

Ready to vote for "Papa Gimme Jimmy."

Proud Grandma and Grandpa, 1997.

Singing to granddaughter Grace, as he always did holding his kids and grandkids.

Enjoying a Family Vacation to Acapulco, 1987.

"If there's one thing I could change about my administration, it would be my hair." – Mayor Griffin

3. Buffalo's Trusted Friend

"In my eyes, and in the eyes of countless Western New Yorkers, there will always be only one mayor—Jim Griffin."
-Ron Anthony, former IBM Executive, NFTA Commissioner, and longtime Mayor Griffin confidant

"He was down to earth; a man of the people and they identified with him. He gave you a straight answer. It may not be what you wanted to hear, but it's what he firmly believed. He was a man of his word."
-Ron Anthony, longtime NFTA Commissioner and Griffin confidant

Sunshine, beer, baseball with old friends at "the House that Jimmy Built." Ron Anthony, Steve McGanka, Mayor Griffin, Ron Armstrong.

51

Alfreda Slominski on Mayor Griffin: *"With him, what you see is what you get. You either hate him or love him. I'm proud to be his friend."*

Mayor Griffin and Erie County Comptroller Alfreda Slominski were named official guides of the State of Colorado on the steps of City Hall.

Mayor Griffin on Alfreda Slominski: *"Some people in the political world have some misgivings because Alfreda has the unique problem of telling the truth. Some people don't like that."*

Aboard the USS Croaker

Ed Rutkowski, Mayor Griffin, Danny Neaverth. 1986

"When Eddie Rutkowski and I go to different meetings, they marvel at how a Democratic mayor and a Republican county executive are friends and buddies and partners. I guess it's not done in other areas and I don't know why, because it should be a natural thing to do."

"He always said and did things that we as other politicians wish we had said and wish we had done, but just didn't have the guts or political courage to do." -Ed Rutkowski

"Yes, I took him around to a few gin mills in South Buffalo and helped him get some votes."
- Mayor Griffin on helping by-that-time State Comptroller Ned Regan get his start in politics in the early 1960s.

Mayor Griffin and Erie County Executive Ned Regan

Working with State Senators Bill Stachowski, Tony Masiello, and Dale Volker

Bob Rich Jr, Bob Rich Sr, Mayor Griffin at Rich Senior's 90th birthday party.

"I always thought Stan was a good guy. He worked with me in the feed mills one summer." –Mayor Griffin on Mayor Makowski

Former Buffalo Mayor Stanley Makowski, Governor Hugh Carey, Mayor Griffin

Mayor Griffin, especially during battles with Governor Carey's successor, Mario Cuomo, always spoke highly of Carey, especially when the governor was helping clean up Delaware Park Lake. (right.)

"We got a winner and a fighter; he's the best man for the job."
-Mayor Griffin on Governor Carey during a re-election bid in 1978

To say Mayor Griffin was not a Mario Cuomo fan would be an understatement. Although the two outwardly carried on a cordial relationship during the Governor's visits to Buffalo from 1983-93, Mayor Griffin was known to openly question Governor Cuomo's abilities.

From Brian Meyer's Book "**The World According to Griffin**":

"There is a singer by the same name. Perry Como might make a better governor than the one we have."
-1991

'I sent a letter to Governor Cuomo today telling him to mind his own business."
– 1984, When the Governor chided the Mayor for backing Republican Ronald Reagan for President instead of Democrat Walter Mondale.

"Governor Cuomo played Class-D baseball. I think it was in the Georgia-Florida League. He must have got hit in the head with a pitched ball if he thinks people enjoy sitting out in the rain."
-1984, on the Governor's downplaying the possibility of a domed baseball stadium in downtown Buffalo.

4. Buffalo's Friend to the Famous

Bob Hope in Buffalo for an Allegheny Airlines event with Mayor Griffin

Right Top: Burt Reynolds visits Mayor Griffin's office as he was in Buffalo filming "Best Friends" in 1983.

Right Bottom: Actor Rip Taylor visits Buffalo City Hall and poses with Mayor Griffin and his staff.

Mayor Griffin with Dabney Coleman and the stars of "Buffalo Bill," the NBC sitcom about a TV show at fictional Buffalo TV station WBFL.

Mayor Griffin with sirens of the silver screen: Above, with Sophia Loren, who he called "a sharp woman who really made you feel at home.". Below, with Ginger Rogers at Shea's.

Olympic Gold Medalist and pro champ Sugar Ray Leonard came to Buffalo to fight Roger Stafford at *The Aud* in 1982, but the Welterweight champ was forced to call off the fight.

While training at the Statler Hilton for the week leading up to the bout, Leonard began to see spots in his vision, and was diagnosed with a detached retina.

One of the nation's most popular athletes in the 80s, Leonard was upset when his injury was described another sign of a "Buffalo jinx."

The Mayor cracking up the champ, at the Statler, 1982.

Mayor Griffin gets a few tips from Olympic Gold Medalist Scott Hamilton at Rotary Rink on Main Street, as he was in Buffalo to skate at "The Stars on Ice" at Memorial Auditorium. The Mayor learned to skate only a month before the downtown rink opened.

Bills Quarterback Jim Kelly endorsed Mayor Griffin in the bid for his last term as Mayor in 1989.

Above: Buffalo Sabres Alumni Morris Titanic (left) and Jr. Sabres player Nick Carone present Mayor Griffin with a jersey. Below, Buffalo Bills Alumni pose with the Mayor and Bills Owner Ralph Wilson on the steps of City Hall.

Mayor Griffin in the foyer of his second floor City Hall office.

Mayor Griffin sits with Buffalo schools Superintendent Eugene Reville as the Rev. Jesse Jackson speaks at Griffin's alma mater, South Park High School.

"The kids are getting a great education in our schools. It's nothing personal between Gene Reville and me. I just wish the taxpayer had a little more concern over what's happening in our schools."

Buffalo Schools Superintendent Eugene Reville said Mayor Griffin was "not a friend of public education in Buffalo." But in 1985, the mayor pointed out funding for schools nearly doubled over his first two terms.

"Take a look again-- $101 million to $196 million in 7 years. I don't think that's being an enemy of education."

County Executive Ed Rutkowski, Senator Alfonse D'Amato, Mayor Griffin, in the Mayor's office

Ed Koch called into Mayor Griffin's radio show on WBEN in the mid-90s, and spoke to the people of Buffalo about Mayor Griffin. "If they are ever so stupid as to throw you out, they'll never get a better mayor, and you a better job.... You tell the truth, and you don't give a rap whether the people like it or not."

Mayor Griffin and Governor Cuomo share a laugh, while former Vice President Mondale seems to be waiting for the punchline, at an event in Buffalo.

Welcoming Senator Edmund Muskie to Buffalo. Ed Rutkowski, Senator Muskie, Henry Nowak, Mayor Griffin, Erie County Democratic Chairman Joe Crangle.

Mayor Griffin shaking hands with Congressman Jim Wright, who would become Speaker of the House, as Congressman Henry Nowak (D), Buffalo, looks on.

"Although he is 6-foot-4, he keeps a low profile. But I usually judge a man by what he has done, and Hank has been, in my opinion, the greatest influence on bringing federal dollars into the City of Buffalo."

-Mayor Griffin on 9-term Buffalo Congressman Henry Nowak

Mayor Griffin and President Carter

VIP DAIS
A Presidential Visit
with
Jimmy Carter
Saturday, October 28, 1978
Buffalo International Airport, Prior Aviation Terminal
Wehrle Drive, (off Cayuga Rd.)
10:00 a.m.
★ **Please use Dais Guest Parking Area**

ADMIT 1

Mayor Griffin, The Country's First Lady Roslyn Carter, and Buffalo's First Lady Margie Griffin

ADMIT ONE
— TO HEAR—
ROSALYN CARTER
"AMERICA'S FIRST LADY"

THURSDAY, JANUARY 31, 1980 – 2 P.M.
— AT —
VILLA MARIA COLLEGE AUDITORIUM
240 Pine Ridge Road, Cheektowaga, N. Y.
18

Mayor Griffin, President Ronald Reagan, and Bishop Edward Head at the dedication of the Santa Maria Apartments on Connecticut Street on Buffalo's West Side.

Mayor Griffin and President Reagan might not have shared the same political party, but they did share a great afternoon together when the President visited Buffalo to dedicate a senior housing complex in 1984.

"He was such a regular guy. A great guy. I really thought the world of the man.

The Republican Party called me and asked me if I would greet the President at the airport, and I said it would be an honor. So I greeted him, and I drove with him in the limousine to the Santa Maria Apartments. He gave a speech, and then we took a walk down Fargo Street, and I was by his side, talking about different things.

Then they said to me, 'would you introduce the President at the luncheon?'

78

Now here's a high school dropout introducing the President of the United States. I introduced him, sat by his side, talked with him some more.

When the luncheon was over, I figured I'd go back to City Hall. The Secret Service said, 'Where you goin'?,' and I said, 'Back to the office.'

They said, 'No you're not. You're going to drive with the President back to the airport.'

So I was in there with Jim Baker, the Secretary of State, Senator D'Amato, and me, and the President. We had some small talk, and the President told me a joke, I told him a joke.

He was looking at all the people waving at the limo and he said, 'Gee whiz, are all those people really out there for me?,' He was a very humble man. That's how I found the man as someone who could talk to anyone, no matter what your status in life, he would go right to your level.

That's how he grew up. His father was on the WPA. The President always had to work for a living; he was a lifeguard through high school and college.

He came from humble beginnings, he lived over a store. I think that set his role in life.

He wasn't any better than anyone else, or any worse than anyone else, and he always treated people on the same level. That showed. There wasn't anything phony about the guy. He was the same whether he was talking to the heads of nations or some 11 year old kid.

You see some guys do that and you know it's phony. With him, there was just an inner thing about him, that you knew he was sincere."

With WBEN's Bill Lacy

5. Doing Right & Having Fun as Mayor

Mary Lou Rath, a mermaid, and Mayor Griffin on the shores of Lake Erie.

"If people have adjectives for (describing) me… What the hell. If they're talking about me, they're leaving someone else alone."

One class-worth of the thousands of school kids who were able to meet the Mayor in his office at City Hall from 1978-1993.

"If we can help any group in Buffalo, we're going to do it. We've done so many things for people, and as long as I'm here, we'll do things for private and public people. That's why we're here. We're here to help the people. The other administrations didn't do that, and the city went to hell in a handbag. If we can help, we will do it."

We don't have underlings in the City of Buffalo. We have team workers in the city. The janitor and the charwoman are just as good as the mayor.

Getting ready for a press conference in the Mayor's Office.

Renaming Main Street "Disco Blvd." outside Record Theatre, in honor of the World's Largest Disco, 1979.

"Johnny Carson was always saying we get blizzards in Buffalo. I don't think he's ever come to Buffalo! We get a lot of negative press… But you talk to someone who gets transferred into Buffalo, and they love it—they don't want to leave. It's a friendly city."

85

"My philosophy is to give an explanation. I think that's what people owe someone. Some people feel my answers are too short or blunt, but I'm not going to change.

"When I don't like people, they know it. I just can't be a phony. Sometimes you make mistakes with people you think are friends, and they turn out they're not. But that's life; there are a lot of Judases in the world."

Having fun: Above, with Mexican hats. Below, with Buffalo weightlifters.

Leading the parade with the circus in town

"I know we've always had an awful lot of wildlife down in the First Ward—I was a part of it—but this is outrageous."

-Mayor Griffin on plans to move the Buffalo Zoo to the waterfront in 1998.

88

Holding a baby chimp from the Buffalo Zoo in the Mayor's Office

"Why should people in jail get a college education when law-abiding people are struggling to send their kids to school?

If the judge says 10 years, then the SOB should serve 10 years.

I'm monitored, and so is everybody else who is elected. Why not the judges? They're getting good money from the public, and nobody grabbed me or them by the neck and told them they had to run. They wanted the job and they should account to the public, the same as the rest of us."

"I think it's time we had civil rights for the elderly lady who gets mugged and has her arm broken while she's trying to hang onto her last five bucks.

My dad's 77, and I worry every day that some asshole is going to hit him over the head and rob him. And I'm the mayor."

To police recruits in 1984:

"We don't expect excellence from you, we demand it. If you're not going to be the best, we don't want you."

"Our city is talking proud because Buffalo is a great place to live and is getting better each day."

In 1986, Mayor Griffin helped Buffalo Police end a standoff when he walked up to a house where a man was holding his three young children hostage with a shot gun.

"It was noon time, it was a cold day in Buffalo, and I heard on the radio that there was a hostage situation on the east side of Buffalo.

This young man, who was unemployed, was holding three of his seven children hostage.

I went to the scene, and I met his wife and mother, who were in the house next door. They were talking to him by the phone, so I asked if I could talk to him.

They said fine, so we talked, and in talking to him, he seemed like an intelligent young man, he was more afraid than anything else, because the SWAT team was running around with their black uniforms and their guns in the ready position.

I felt the situation could be handled without any bloodshed, so after talking to him, I asked him if it would be alright if I come in and talk to him face-to-face, that AT&T was the only ones making any money off of us talking on the phone.

He said it was fine, so when I went in the home, he had a shot gun and about 300 rounds of ammunition, but the one thing I noticed was he was just about finished changing the diapers on one of his children.

So I figured, this guy isn't going to harm anybody. As I said, he was more afraid than anything else.

We started talking, and I mentioned that I would help him try to get a job, and I said, 'you don't have to worry, no one's going to arrest you. In fact, I said I'll drive you home in the mayor's car.'

One thing led to another, and he threw the shot gun out the door and got rid of the ammunition.

92

As soon as we got out the door, I said, 'Well, let's get home.' I kept my promise and drove him back to his mother's house where he was staying.

I mentioned to the authorities that there was no harm done to his wife or the mother of his children, so there were no charges.

But the story doesn't end there. We got him a job, and he worked on it for a few years."

Mayor Griffin and Bishop Edward D. Head at St. Joseph Cathedral

Tom Griffin, far right, shares a laugh with his brother after someone handed him a beer during the St. Patrick's Day parade.

"People say, 'Jimmy, make friends and forget it.' But you're never going to see me make a friend of an enemy. I want the enemy over there where I can see him. And I am never going to change.

-Mayor Griffin

Jimmy Slattery went from First Ward kid to international light heavyweight champion and superstar to down-on-his-luck drunk working for the city parks department over the course of two decades.

He made what would be tens of millions in today's money, but during the Depression, he gave most of it away-- buying shoes for an entire school, or coal to heat an entire street.

His fists made him famous, but his heart made him a legend. Mayor Griffin always listed Slattery as one of his heroes:

"He lived a full life, and if he came back tomorrow, he'd probably do the same thing. That was his life, and boy, you can't hate a guy for that."

"I've always been outspoken. Because if you're not, well-- I never needed a job that much that I had to take anybody's baloney."

6. Half-a-Century on the Campaign Trail

Mayor Griffin, on his start in politics:

"I was in a tavern, as I usually was in those days—Kennedy's at the foot of Catherine Street. Frankie Hahn was tending bar. They'd passed my name again on the Civil Service list and there wasn't a thing I could do about it. So I decided then and there I was going to change the system. I ran against Kupsy Kolodiej for 8th Ward Supervisor. I got beat by 150 votes, but I guess they knew I was around."

Two years later, in 1961, he ran independently for Ellicott District Councilman. He won the primary, and then the general election, while working third shift on the railroad, sleeping for a few hours, then ringing doorbells starting at 10am. He served two terms.

Front row: Councilmen Makowski, Griffin, Santa Lucia, Ramunno, Cegielski, Szudzik, Dudzick, Mitchell, Morrisey, Mahoney, Petrella, Buyers, Benzow, and Lyman. Top Row: Council President Chester Gorski, and City Clerk Stanley Molik, c.1962.

Griffin was elected to 6 terms in the State Senate, starting in 1966.

"I was an independent- or an asshole—depending on your point of view. I really got along better with the Republicans than the Democrats."

Above: Councilman Griffin speaking with constituents on the campaign trail in the Ellicott District. Below: Senator Griffin shown to his office door in Albany.

Jim & Margie Griffin on the campaign trail

Jim Griffin announced his candidacy for Mayor of Buffalo in February, 1977. He lost the Democratic primary in September, but ran in November on the Conservative line.

The race was close in 1977, and Griffin didn't speak on Election Night as Mayor-Elect until well after midnight, when he said, in part, *"I have no doubts in my mind whatsoever that this city can pull itself together. Buffalo is just like it always has been; a city of good neighbors. And we're going to make it better.*

January 1, 1978- Mrs. & Mayor Griffin, moments after being sworn in Common Council chambers

"One of Margie and my favorite songs is 'Camelot.' The song speaks of a place where everything is beautiful and where anyone would want to live. It is a place of hopes and dreams. One of the lines of the song says that 'there's a legal limit to the snow here. The winter is forbidden 'til December and exits March the second on the dot.'

"Now, I can't promise that it will only snow from December to March. What I am promising is that the decisions that are made and the actions that are taken by this administration will be dedicated to what is best for all the residents of the City of Buffalo.

"Together we will make Buffalo a place where anyone would want to come to live, work, and raise a family. Together, we can have a Buffalo—to quote "Camelot" again—about which is said that..

'In short, there's simply not a more congenial spot for happ'ly ever aftering.'"

-From Mayor Griffin's first inaguaral address, 1978

"I campaigned on very simple ideas. Everybody said, 'You've got a simple solution to everything.' Well, that's the way life is. You can't make it complex.

If the people in a neighborhood say they want a stop sign, that stop sign goes up. I don't wait for surveys.

If I think there should be more policemen on the streets, I don't wait for FBI statistics.

I believe in the simple way of doing things. More than experts, we need people with common sense in government."

"I like this job. The Senate was easier; you could always rationalize your vote. This has 100 times more responsibility, and either you're right or wrong."

"It's shoe leather, and that doesn't cost a lot of money."

Mayor Griffin always ran very thrifty campaigns, going so far as spending weeks making ice cubes at home for campaign events to avoid the cost of buying it. It wasn't cash, but meeting and connecting with people that was most important in a campaign.

Said Mayor Griffin of one of his many no-frills fundraisers:

"It's $20. No split clubs, no nothin'. Beer, pizza, pretzels, and a lot of laughs. Margie says maybe I can use some of my First Communion money from back in 1936 at St. Brigid's."

"I've been running this way since 1959. I never change."

"Some guys let power go to their heads. I hope it hasn't changed me. I've tried to keep my old friends, in and out of politics. Power is something God gives you, and you have responsibility to use it in a certain way."

Irish & Honorary Irish: Chuck Poth, Mayor Griffin, Stan Buczkowski, and George Gould

"Nobody has more loyal supporters than me."

"The guy that gets all the guff is the mayor. I'm here to take the blame. I'm here to take the criticism. That's the way it's going to be so long as I'm mayor. I think people like that."

"I do step on toes. I might be vicious at times. If you had my job, you'd do the same."

An animated Mayor Griffin with then-WGRZ-TV reporter Don Postles

What's more Buffalo than cheering for the Bills and Jimmy Griffin...

"*I will complete 16 years as mayor on Dec. 31, 1993. This is the longest tenure which any mayor has served in Buffalo's history. This job is a great job. We are able to help people. We help build homes, create jobs in the private sector, fill jobs, both permanent and seasonal in city government and also provide summer work for thousands of kids so they can earn money for school and clothes and have a few bucks for some fun times.*"

In 1996, Mayor Griffin ran a primary campaign for President against Bill Clinton in New Hampshire. He came in seventh place, with 278 votes.

On why he ran for and won the South District Common Council seat in 2003 at the age of 74:

"What the hell, you know... This city and South Buffalo, as nice as they are, they need some competition.

"Things are tough, and we all know it. The way I see it, the glass is half full, and we can make a difference. And that's why we won."

In March, 2005, Mayor Griffin announced his resignation from the Common Council, and closed his final press release as an elected official with a sentence that sums it all up.

"Thanks for one hell of a ride."

7. The Sportsman

"Some people think I might not have one-- but I gotta keep my heart going."

-Mayor Griffin on his daily exercise regimen

Mayor Griffin regularly played handball and golf during his time as mayor.

With Buffalo's own PGA Tour golfer Jim Thorpe.

117

Golf was always a time for Mayor Griffin to relax with friends and family.

Above: The Mayor and his grandson John Tomczak enjoying some golf

Right: Pat Rubino, Tom Griffin, Ed Rutkowski, Mayor Griffin and Tom Griffin, kneeling.

Above: With Buffalo Sabres owner Seymour Knox on the ice at Memorial Auditorium.
Below: With Buffalo Bills owner Ralph C. Wilson, Jr.

The start of Mayor Griffin's love affair with baseball:
"I remember when they used to have field days out at Delaware Park. That's when they had all the races. I ran for St. Brigid's from 3rd grade on. I'll never forget, they had Frank the Elephant there one day, they had them out from the zoo. We were all gathered around Frank, and I looked down and saw a glove. A first baseman's glove. Some kid must have dropped it, and we never found the owner. So that was it, my first glove."

"I played with St. Brigid's, Our Lady of Victory High School, and Army ball. When I got out, I played with Erie County Tech and Muny ball."

Rarely did Mayor Griffin pass up the chance to put on a glove and head out to the mound to throw out a ceremonial opening pitch, either at War Memorial Stadium (above), or at Pilot Field.

The many photos of the Mayor pitching proved helpful to sculptor William Koch, who created the Mayor Griffin statue outside the Home of the Buffalo Bisons, formerly Pilot Field now Coca-Cola Field.

8. The Builder

Mayor Griffin considered Buffalo's unprecedented development during his time in office as his greatest achievement as mayor.

"I believe it's our economic development. I get an awful lot of satisfaction, because these are numbers that no one is going to equal.

"The affordable housing program, my mother and father never owed a house, so that's key.

"Pilot Field. That's great. First of all, no one thought we'd be able to bring baseball back to Buffalo. But we did, and we brought it back at a place where everyone was scared to death to go, War Memorial Stadium. We never had one incident over at War Memorial Field. Then we said we were going to build a stadium in downtown Buffalo and everybody, including the Buffalo News, thought we were nuts. But we did it.

"The Theatre District is another great thing. We've got an eight-screen movie theatre downtown, we got a TGI Fridays. They never put a TGI Fridays and a movie theatre in a downtown area.

"I won't say proud, but I'll say I'm happy with what we've done in the city."

"When you're broke, life's problems are bigger. When you can't reach down into your pocket and pull out a dollar or five dollars, then all of your problems seem to get bigger. Work is the best therapy that anybody can get. And that's my principal job as the mayor of the city of Buffalo."

Not only did Mayor Griffin have an overall vision for the development of Buffalo's neighborhoods, downtown, and waterfront, but he'd often get his hands dirty—literally-- with hundreds of ground breakings, and figuratively by personally negotiating many development plans.

Mayor Griffin's passion for baseball and passion for revitalizing downtown Buffalo and the waterfront all culminated with Pilot Field, the $42 million baseball park which opened in 1988.

Pilot Air Freight signed on for naming rights of the downtown ballpark, only to default on payments in 1995. Since opening in 1988, the ballpark has been known as Pilot Field, NorthAmeriCare Park, Dunn Tire Park, and now, Coca-Cola Field.

"We were pretty far down in back in those days, but I knew baseball could help this city."

Right Top: Mindy & Bob Rich, Governor Cuomo, and Mayor Griffin on Opening Day at Pilot Field, 1988.

Right Below: Once the Bisons moved out of War Memorial Stadium, Mayor Griffin moved forward with plays for the redevelopment of the stadium as a youth sports complex.

"I'm a guy that wants to get things done. I don't want to keep planning for three or five years and not see anything. I like to get something where people can see it, and where we can make a success, because success breeds success."

Though most of the work and planning was done during the Stanley Makowski administration, Mayor Griffin joined County Executive Ned Regan in cutting the ribbon on the new convention center in 1978.

"You aren't going to see big firms like Bethlehem and Republic hiring thousands of people like they used to. The future is in little firms."

"We are going to develop this city block-by-block with the help of private enterprise, professionals, and the banks."

"We're getting rid of the dirty bookstores downtown. We don't want downtown to have a honky-tonk atmosphere. We had that years ago, and that's what drove people out of Buffalo."

"I'm going to keep on doing the same thing I've done before, and if I have to step on toes, you know I'm doing it for your benefit. I think that's what the mayor is supposed to do. He's supposed to show leadership, he's supposed to say no once in a while, and he's supposed to step on toes."

"Paul Snyder, he'll come shooting at the hip. He'll say Buffalo is one of the greatest places in the country to invest money. And those are the kind of statements you like to hear. "

"Here's a guy who broke his neck for this city, and people just don't realize it. There were deals that I never would have touched if it hadn't been for him. It was always, 'Aw, c'mon Frank. The city needs it.'"-
Frank Ciminelli on Mayor Griffin

Mayor Griffin's leadership on the development of the Hilton (Adam's Mark) Hotel, the Erie Basin Marina and the surrounding area is widely recognized as the forerunner and basis for the development that has taken place at Buffalo's inner harbor since.

I.   Epilogue

James D. Griffin 1929-2008

Less than a year after his final campaign, a spirited primary run for
Erie County Executive, Mayor Griffin died May 25, 2008. He was
diagnosed with Creutzfeldt–Jakob disease, a rare degenerative
neurological disorder hallmarked by rapidly progressing dementia.

Since his death, Mayor Griffin has been honored with the naming of
the plaza at Washington and Swan Streets outside of Coca-Cola Field
as "James D. Griffin Plaza," honoring his dogged determination in
getting the ballpark built.

Griffin's family and the Buffalo Bisons have also worked to honor the
mayor's memory, and to raise awareness for the family of diseases
which took his life.

On August 17, 2012, friends and family of Mayor Griffin and the
Buffalo Bisons unveiled a bronze statue of the mayor throwing out an
opening pitch, as he had done so many times for the Bisons.

Longtime friends and supporters of Mayor Griffin gather around his likeness as the statue was dedicated in 2012.

In 2013, the Griffin children, friends, family, and once again the Buffalo Bisons joined once again in honoring Mayor Griffin's memory, this time with the *Run Jimmy Run Charity 5k.*

Proceeds of the race benefited the Alzheimer's Association of Western New York, which helped Mayor Griffin and his family during his final days.

During his years as mayor, the annual *Run, Jimmy Run!* events raised thousands of dollars for some of the Griffin family's favorite charities.

In memory and in honor of the mayor, several Buffalo charities will benefit from the sale of this book.

About the Author

A child of South Buffalo in the 1980s, Steve Cichon is understandably a Jimmy Griffin fan. His Grandma Cichon surprised him once as a little boy with an autographed "Griffin for Mayor" bumper sticker, and through the years, his Grandpa Coyle had a quite a few "Vote Griffin" signs stapled to his front porch spindles.

As a producer and reporter at WBEN Radio, WIVB-TV, and WNSA/Empire Sports Network for two decades, Steve would often add colorful memories and insights to any story by making the always accessible former mayor a part of the stories he telling.

Cichon is the author and publisher of two other books, *The Complete History of Parkside* and *Irv! Buffalo Anchorman: the Irv, Rick, and Tom Story*, and is also the editor-in-chief of *www.staffannouncer.com*, a website devoted to the collection, preservation, and sharing of Western New York's pop culture history.

He left WBEN Radio as News Director in 2013 to found Buffalo Stories LLC, where he is able to help individuals, non-profits, and small businesses tell and profit from stories through writing books, producing video documentaries, and creating web-based blogs and video.

A winner of dozens of Associated Press reporting excellence awards and of *Buffalo Business First's 40 Under 40* award in 2010, Cichon has been described by the *Buffalo News* as "the go-to man for memories of all things local."

Steve and his wife Monica Cichon live in Buffalo's Parkside neighborhood, where she serves as community association president, and he has served as parish council president at St. Mark Roman Catholic Church. Between official duties around the neighborhood, they've been slowly renovating their 1909 EB Green American four-square home, which they share with SPCA mutt Willow.

Acknowledgements

Through more than 50 years in public life, hundreds of photographers sent Mayor Griffin thousands of photos. We are thankful for those who captured the moments of Jim Griffin's life on film, and were willing to share those snapshots in time with the Mayor. As you've read here, the images of his public life has helped his family tell the story of his private life. Thank you.

In preparing this book, I read thousands of news articles from the Buffalo News, The Buffalo Courier-Express, and the Mayor's columns in The Metro Community News. I also watched and listened to dozens of hours of radio and TV news coverage of Mayor Griffin from WGR, WBEN, WEBR, WBFO, WKBW, WGRZ-TV, WIVB-TV, and WKBW-TV. Books by Brian Meyer, Dave McKinley, and Mike Rizzo were also great references.

Maureen Griffin-Tomczak, Megan Griffin, and Tom Griffin and their families not only care about and understand their father's legacy, but also very deeply care about what that legacy can do to help people now. To see them quietly working hard in their parents' honor on a host of different projects-- including this book— shows that they care about this community and the people of this community as much as any Griffin ever has. And that's saying something. They each also read through drafts of this book to find errors in fact and in language.

My wife Monica read and re-read this book, green highlighter in hand. Her copy editing of my book projects are the only time in our marriage when I wholly appreciate her correcting me. This is the third book she has lived through, and you are reading it now only because of her saintly patience. Fanks, sweetie pie.

Marty Biniasz, Brian Meyer, Greg Bauch, Chrissy Casilio-Bluhm, Krystyna Karstedt, Lindsay Truesdell, Fr. John Mack, Howard Goldman, John Bisci, Rich Wolf, Fr. Marty Moleski, Bernie Wagner, Tom Ziobro, Al Wallack, Libby Maeder, Kateri Ewing, Mike & Mary O'Sullivan, Fr. Tom Ribits, Haley Bujeda, Braydon Becker, Gianna Becker, and Willow the Dog have all provided material and emotional support beyond their knowledge and comprehension. Thanks.